To Sunny Alexandria

"I'm so grateful to have grown up in a church where I learned about missions and missionaries—but I never heard this story! I'm so glad to know it now and I'm so glad that this book will make Maria's story known."

NANCY GUTHRIE, Author and Bible teacher

"Maria Fearing was a remarkable woman with a beautiful story. Karen Ellis tells that story simply and effectively—this is an inspiring missionary tale for children and also for their parents!"

SARAH EEKHOFF ZYLSTRA, Senior Writer, The Gospel Coalition

"This is a wonderful account of how God has used a remarkable woman to bring the good news of the kingdom to many children in need. We pray her story will inspire countless others to answer the call to the Great Commission."

LLOYD KIM, Coordinator of Mission to the World (Presbyterian Church in America)

"Karen Ellis was already a hero of mine when she first introduced me to Maria Fearing—who quickly joined the pantheon. Hers is such an often-forgotten voice, and I am so excited to see her story in this engaging, accessible format! Karen's gifts as a storyteller and an encourager meld beautifully in this tribute to Maria."

JASMINE HOLMES, Author, *Carved in Ebony* and *Mother to Son*; Co-Host, The Gospel Coalition's *Let's Talk* podcast

Maria Fearing
© K.A. Ellis 2023
Illustrated by Isobel Muñoz | Design and Art Direction by André Parker
Series Concept by Laura Caputo-Wickham
Published in association with the literary agency of THE GATES GROUP.
"The Good Book For Children" is an imprint of The Good Book Company Ltd.
thegoodbook.com | thegoodbook.co.uk | thegoodbook.com.au
thegoodbook.co.nz | thegoodbook.co.in
ISBN: 9781784988265 | Printed in India

thegoodbook
for children

Do Great Things for God

Maria Fearing

The Girl Who Dreamed of Distant Lands

K.A. Ellis

Illustrated by Isabel Muñoz

Little Maria* dreamed of another world.

*Pronounced "Mar-EYE-ah"

She heard the grown-ups speak of a far-off land where there were many people like her—but she had never seen this place, nor did she know how to get there.

She only knew that it was an entire ocean away and that it was a continent called Africa. So far away!

AFRICA

Maria heard that Africa was a place of extraordinary people like kings and queens, and everyday people like hunters and gatherers, weavers and traders, and, of course, mommies and daddies.

The people of this faraway place did their best to protect their children.

But others had come and taken their children over the seas, and sold them in faraway places whose names were strange to their ears: places like Alabama, where Maria lived.

As years passed, the mommies and daddies thought often about their missing children. Would they ever see them again?

In their secret late-night forest church near her Alabama plantation, Maria and her friends heard about the God who created the heavens and the earth, the stars, the sun and the seas, and all that's on and in them. She heard stories about God's people of all colors, who adorned his world.

When this great, grand God called his special ones "Mine," she knew that she, too, was his special one, for he had captured her heart and filled it with hope.

One night, as the fireflies danced, little Maria wondered if God could take her to the far-off land called Africa. She knew that even though it was forbidden to leave the plantation where she was enslaved, nothing was too difficult for her God.

If he would make her free, she could see many far-off places with her own eyes.

Oh, how she longed to be free!

Years later, when Maria was a grown woman, a man galloped up the road on a fast and majestic horse.

The dust of freedom fairly flew from its hooves.

LIBERTY

The horseman told Maria and all her people great news—she and all her people were no longer slaves!

Maria left that Alabama plantation with her feet itching to travel. She already knew her choice:

"I will go to Africa!"

But where in Africa? Such an enormous place—
more than three times the size of the United States!

And how would she get there? It was a whole
ocean away! Getting there would have to be a
God-made plan...

Maria made and sold dresses to the women in town.
She saved every penny, and she prayed.

And one day, she met a young missionary
preacher and his wife who were journeying
to a place in Africa called Congo!

They invited Maria to join them and tell people there of God's great love. Maria said, "Yes!" and set sail with them across the ocean on an enormous boat!

The journey took a long time, but at last,
Maria reached Africa's shores.

God had opened every impossible door.

But sadness awaited Maria. Congo was ruled by a cruel king named Leopold II. He commanded his men to sell little orphan boys and girls into slavery, just like Maria had been sold as a little girl.

God didn't like King Leopold's cruelty... and now Maria knew why God had brought her to Congo.

Maria often stood up to these powerful men with their angry faces and their huge, sharp knives. She traded scissors, salt, and strings of fine beads to set the children free. Then the children came to live with her in her home.

Whenever the angry men pounded on their door, Maria and the children huddled together while she reminded them of God's promises in a whisper.

"Be calm now, children. Let's remember what God says in his word to anyone who trusts in him:

"'I will protect him because he knows my name.
When he calls out to me, I will answer him;
I will be with him in trouble.
I will rescue him and give him honor.
I will satisfy him with a long life
and show him my salvation.'" (Psalm 91 v 14-16)

Maria spent many years gathering children into her home until she was an old woman. Free and safe with her, for many years children fluttered in and out of her African home like busy little butterflies.

She taught the children to live with dignity—dressmaking, farming, cooking, woodworking, reading, doing math... loving God first, and then their neighbors as themselves.

With her other missionary friends, Maria helped put the Bible into the language of these little ones for the first time. It took many years of hard work, but finally, the children could read about God with their whole God-made African being!

Maria loved the children in the way that Jesus loves people, as her very own.

And the children loved Maria, so they gave her a special name: Mama wa Mputu.

Can you guess what this special name meant?

In the children's language, it meant "Mother from Far Away." This name meant the world to Maria.

It proved that, all along, God had meant to bring her across an entire ocean just to offer many, many children a peaceful, loving, hope-filled home—a home with Jesus in this life and a home with him forever in glory.

MAMA WA MPUTU

Maria Fearing

1838 – 1937

"When [she] calls out to me, I will answer [her];

I will be with [her] in trouble."

Psalm 91 v 15 (CSB)

Questions to Think About

1. Which part of Maria's story did you like best?

2. Maria remembered that God promises in the Bible, *When someone calls out to me, I will answer them; I will be with them in trouble.* How does this encourage you to speak to God? Is there any trouble you are facing at the moment, or anything that is making you feel worried? You can talk to God about it and know that he is with you!

3. Maria and her friends worked hard to make sure the children she cared for had a Bible that they could read in their own language. If you have a Bible in your language, how does that make you feel? When and how can you read it each day?

4. What ideas does Maria's story give you about how you might serve Jesus when you are older?

5. What is one truth about God that you'd like to remember from this story?

Maria Fearing

July 26, 1838: Maria was born near Gainesville, Alabama. Her parents were called Mary and Jesse. They were enslaved and forced to work on a plantation owned by a man named William O. Winston.

Maria worked as a slave in William O. Winston's home. She was a nanny and a house servant.

1865: At the end of the American Civil War, all enslaved people in the United States were set free. Maria was 27.

Maria learned to read and write and became a teacher. She worked at a school in a town called Anniston.

May 1894: When she was 56, Maria went to the Belgian Congo (now called the Democratic Republic of the Congo) with William Henry Sheppard. She sold her own house so that she had enough money for the journey. When their ship reached the Congo, they had to travel 1,200 miles to Luebo, where they lived.

The Congo was ruled by King Leopold II of Belgium. His soldiers treated the people brutally. Maria worked as a teacher, and she also helped translate the Bible into Baluba-Lulua. She traveled round the villages, telling people about Jesus. She bought many people out of slavery and set up the Pantops Home for Girls in Luebo for girls who were orphaned or had been kidnapped and enslaved. Around 50 girls lived there at a time.

1915: At the age of 77, Maria retired as a missionary and returned to the United States. She taught in a school in Selma, Alabama.

May 23, 1937: Maria died aged 99.

NORTH
AMERICA

USA

EUROP

SOUTH
AMERICA

World Map

Where in the world
did Maria's story
take place?

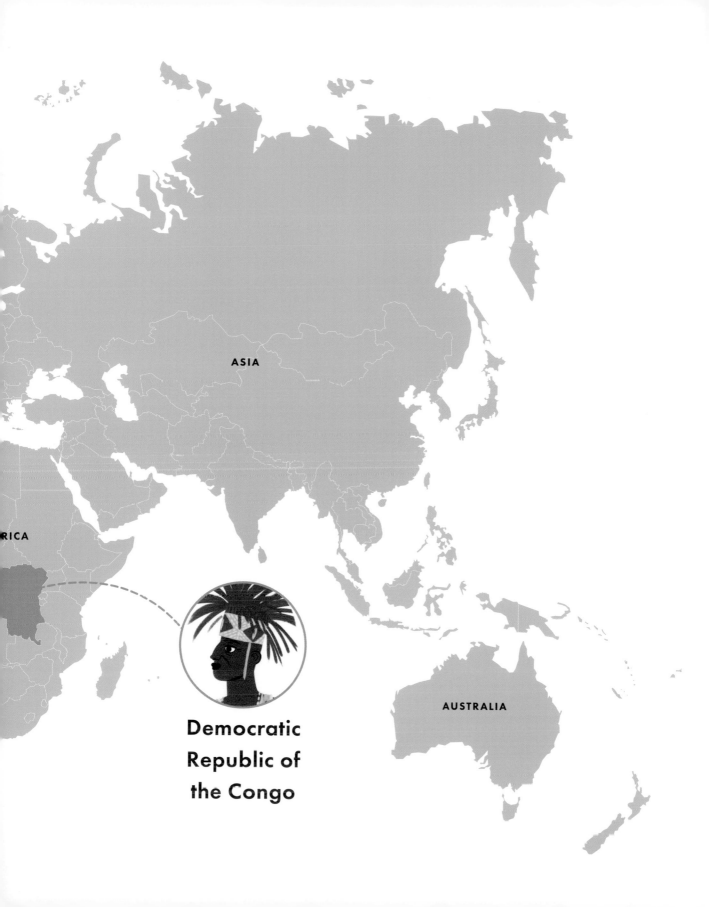

ASIA

RICA

AUSTRALIA

Democratic Republic of the Congo

Interact with Maria's Story!

8-11s

Biography Report for
Maria Fearing
(Pronounced Mar-EYE-ah)

By: _____

My favorite thing about Maria:
_____
_____

Person from the Bible Maria reminds me of:
_____

A question I would ask Maria:
_____
_____
_____

Three words I would use to describe Maria:
1. _____
2. _____
3. _____

Remember this Verse Maria Loved
"I will _____ him because he
_____ my _____."
Psalm 91 v 14
Can you say it 3 times without looking?

• PASSPORT •
Maria Fearing
Year of Birth:
Hometown:
Job Title:
(Draw a Portrait)

Search Online to Find:
Ask an adult about doing this together!

Where in Congo* did Maria live?
What did she do there?
_____
_____

How long did Maria spend in Congo?
_____

What kinds of things did the girls who lived
in and attended Maria's school, called
Pantops, learn to do?
_____
_____
_____

*This region has sometimes been one country, and other times two. It has had many different names. To keep it simple, we call the region Maria served in "Congo."

1

Tell Maria's story in your own words. You can even pretend you
are Maria and say "I", thinking about how she might feel.

_____
_____
_____
_____
_____
_____
_____
_____
_____
_____
_____

Can you put these events in order? Number the boxes from 1 to 5.

☐ Maria moved to Africa.

☐ Maria worked as a Bible translator.

☐ Maria learned to read and write.

☐ Maria established the Pantops Home for Girls.

☐ Maria became a teacher in Calhoun County.

Family Activity: Think about the new name the children of Congo gave to Maria. Now, look up a few of God's
names in the Bible. Like Maria's name, those names tell us something about God. What do you think they say?

2

What Are 8 Things You Liked about Maria's Story?

1.
2.
3.
4.
5.
6.
7.
8.

Remember this Verse Maria Loved

"I will protect him because he knows my name."

Psalm 91 v 14

Can you say it all by yourself? ☐

Family Activity: Think about the new name the children of Congo gave to Maria. Now, look up a few of God's names in the Bible. Like Maria's name, those names tell us something about God. What do you think they say?

4-7s

All About

Maria Fearing
(Pronounced Mar-EYE-ah)

By: _____

My Drawing of Maria

Where did Maria grow up?

Where did Maria dream to go?

What Did Maria Do When...   Circle the Answer

Her people were freed from slavery	Decided to stay in Alabama **OR** Decided to go to Africa
She needed to raise money to go to Africa	Made and sold dresses **OR** Opened a bakery
Missionaries asked her to join them in Congo*	Raised more funds **OR** Said, "yes!"
She went to Africa	Became a teacher **OR** Rescued children from slavery

*This region has sometimes been one country, and other times two. It has had many different names. To keep it simple, we call the region Maria served in "Congo."

Download free resources at

thegoodbook.com/kids-resources

Do Great Things for God

Inspiring Biographies for Young Children

Corrie ten Boom
The Courageous Woman and the Secret Room
Laura Caputo-Wickham
Illustrated by Isabel Muñoz

Betsey Stockton
The Girl With a Missionary Dream
Laura Caputo-Wickham
Illustrated by Eunji Jung

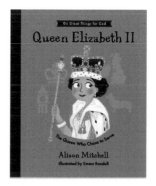

Queen Elizabeth II
The Queen Who Chose to Serve
Alison Mitchell
Illustrated by Emma Randall

Gladys Aylward
The Little Woman With a Big Dream
Laura Caputo-Wickham
Illustrated by Jess Rose

Betty Greene
The Girl Who Longed to Fly
Laura Caputo-Wickham
Illustrated by Héloïse Mab

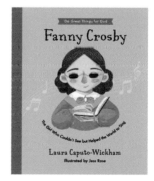

Fanny Crosby
The Girl Who Couldn't See but Helped the World to Sing
Laura Caputo-Wickham
Illustrated by Jess Rose

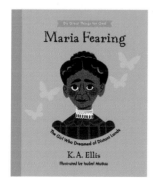

Maria Fearing
The Girl Who Dreamed of Distant Lands
K. A. Ellis
Illustrated by Isabel Muñoz

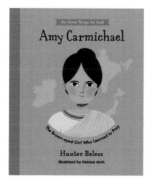

Amy Carmichael
The Brown-eyed Girl Who Learned to Pray
Hunter Beless
Illustrated by Héloïse Mab

Helen Roseveare
The Doctor Who Kept Going No Matter What
Laura Caputo-Wickham
Illustrated by Cecilia Messina